Mel Bay's Deluxe

ACCORDION METHOD

By Frank Zucco

1 2 3 4 5 6 7 8 9 0

CONTENTS

ADJUSTING THE STRAPS

The height of the accordion is very important but can vary with different individuals. Your instructor can adjust the shoulder straps for the proper height. The bass straps should be adjusted so that the palm of the left hand rests flat against the baseboard grill at all times. This is especially important when pulling the bellow outward.

THE BELLOW

Before going on, let us consider the very heart of the accordion, the bellow. Controlling the bellow of the accordion is very similar to developing good bowing techniques on the violin or to developing proper breath control on a wind instrument. Having the shoulder straps properly adjusted is very important in developing bellow control. With the help of your instructor, put the accordion on and insert the left hand in the bass strap (all five fingers should be inserted). Unsnap the accordion at the top and bottom. With the thumb, depress the air button in a "fan-shape motion." Slowly open and close the bellow several times in order to thoroughly get acquainted with the outward motion. Whenever you start an exercise or tune, always start the bellow in an outward motion. Never change the direction of the bellow while sounding a tone.

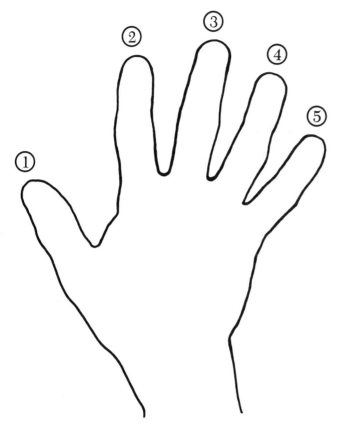

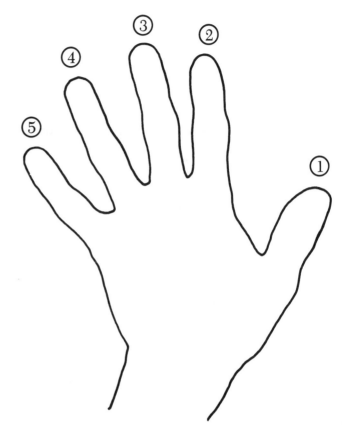

LEFT HAND

RIGHT HAND

LEFT HAND
ON THE BASS BUTTONS

RIGHT HAND
ON THE KEYBOARD

THE ACCORDION AND ITS PARTS

Shoulder Strap

Bellows

Bellow Snap

Black & White Keys

Air Button

Grill

Bass Buttons

Bass Strap

NOTES AND KEYS

Students can start playing on their very first lesson by using a combination of rote letter names and finger numbers. Assuming that the student is beginning on a twelve bass accordion, the first three white keys are C-D-E. C is the white key which appears before the two black keys. D is the white key between the two black keys and E is the white key after the two black keys. Look at the drawing for the location of these three notes.

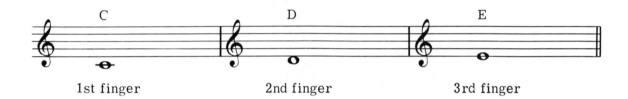

1st finger   2nd finger   3rd finger

HELPFUL HINTS BEFORE PLAYING
(Finding The C Key Without Looking)

Practice the following procedure at a sitting position. The bellow should be snapped closed. Open your right hand and rest it on your knee. Slowly raise your right hand and grasp the first two black keys between the first and third fingers. In so doing, place the first finger on the C key and the second finger between the two black keys on the D key. The third finger, then, should rest on the E key. Master this movement before starting to play. When playing, the hand may be moved outward and away from the black keys. When we use the black keys, as an aid in finding the proper white keys, we are using a procedure called "feel and touch." Mastering this technique will prevent the student from looking down at the keyboard too often. "Feel and touch" technique can be a great help to all players, especially when making larger skips involving fourth, fifth, sixth, seventh intervals and even octaves. Students should maintain a good hand position. The fingers should be curved, the elbow should be out slightly and the right hand should be parallel with the black keys.

THE C POSITION

In this position, the first finger (thumb) determines the name of the position. Place your first finger on C and play the first five notes: C-1, D-2, E-3, F-4, G-5. This is referred to as the C position. If you would place your thumb on the D key, that would be called the D position. The following studies have been written in the C position (thumb on the C note).

THE TREBLE CLEF SIGN

This sign is called the treble clef sign and it means to play the right hand, or the piano keys.

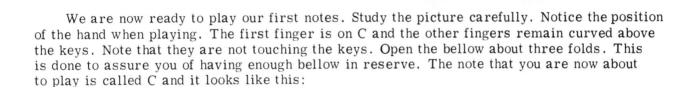

We are now ready to play our first notes. Study the picture carefully. Notice the position of the hand when playing. The first finger is on C and the other fingers remain curved above the keys. Note that they are not touching the keys. Open the bellow about three folds. This is done to assure you of having enough bellow in reserve. The note that you are now about to play is called C and it looks like this:

1st finger

WHOLE NOTE

This type of note is called a whole note. It has a duration of four counts.

LET'S PLAY

With a steady and even outward motion, play the following study. Be careful not to play too loud.

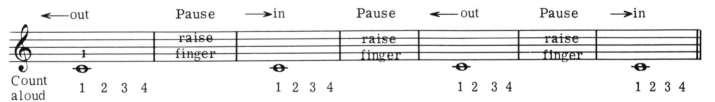

THINGS TO REMEMBER
(Find The C Key Without Looking)

Raise only the finger (thumb) at the end of the four counts. The hand and fingers should remain over the keyboard at all times. Master the above study before continuing. Remember: controlling the bellow is very important.

D
A NEW NOTE

The next key up from the C key is called D. Proceed in the same manner as on page 6. Find the two black keys. The second finger may remain slightly between the two black keys. The first, third, fourth and fifth fingers should remain curved slightly above the keys. Remember - the D note that we will be playing is also a whole note and should receive four counts. It looks like this:

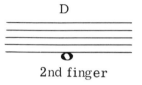

D

2nd finger

With the bellow slightly opened at the top, proceed in the same manner as on page 6. Remember to strive for a steady inward and outward bellow motion. Do not play too loud.

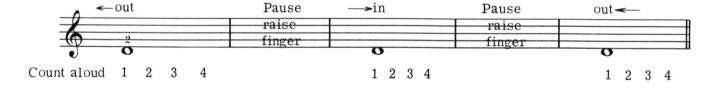

Count aloud   1 2 3 4   1 2 3 4   1 2 3 4

E
ANOTHER NEW NOTE

E is the next key up from the D key. Find the E key in the same manner by the aid of the two black keys. The third finger should rest on the E key. The other fingers should remain in the appropriate position but not touching the other keys. Remember, the E note that we will be playing is also a whole note and it receives four counts. It looks like this:

E

3rd finger

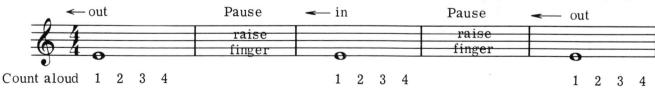

Count aloud   1 2 3 4   1 2 3 4   1 2 3 4

PLAYING WITHOUT STOPPING

The following studies should be played in a strict tempo. Before proceeding on, check your hand position. Are the fingers curved? Is the elbow out slightly? Is the right hand parallel with the black keys? The hand should remain loose. Make sure that it does not feel stiff and rigid. Only the fingers are raised and lowered. <u>Remember</u>: only the finger that is playing should touch the key. All the other fingers should remain raised above the keys.

TOP OF THE BELLOW SLIGHTLY OPENED
First Finger C

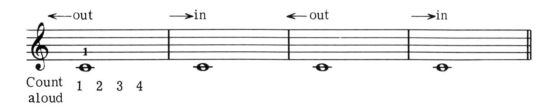

Count aloud   1 2 3 4

Second Finger D

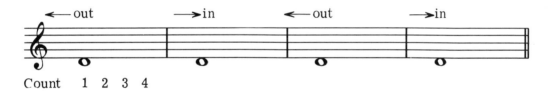

Count   1 2 3 4

Third Finger E

Count

Check Point

Try to produce a steady and even tone when opening and closing the bellow. Never change the direction of the bellow when playing a note. Complete all four counts before you raise the finger. Change the direction of the bellow after the four counts and continue onto the next note. Remember: the bellow is the very heart of the accordion.

MORE ABOUT THE RIGHT HAND FINGERS

The preceeding studies and the studies which will be following have been written for development of the first, second and third fingers. These fingers are the strongest and the most agile. Because of this, the student will be able to concentrate more on bellow control, counting and correct hand positioning. The letter names have purposely been omitted on the following studies. The student should begin learning the actual names of the notes. The fourth and fifth fingers on the right hand will be introduced on the following pages.

Charge

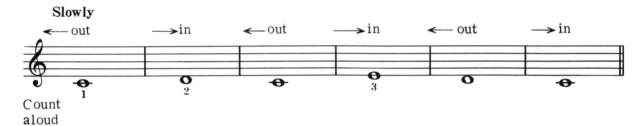

Over the top

Success

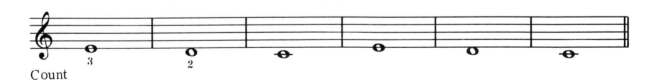

Combining both hands too soon could be a problem for some students. Studying the above studies in addition to the introduction of a new note on the preceeding page should give the student enough time and practice and knowledge of bellow playing control.

THE TYPES OF NOTES

Quarter   Half   Dotted Half   Whole

The type of note will will indicate the length of its sound.

♩	This is a quarter note the head is solid it has a stem.	♩	= 1 - Beat a quarter note will receive one beat or one count.

♩	This is a half note the head is hallow it has a stem.	♩	= 2 - Beats a half note will receive two beats or counts.

THE RULE OF THE DOT

A dot placed after a note increases its time valve by one half.

♩.	This a dotted half note its head is hallow-it has a a stem and a dot.	♩.	= 3 Beats a dotted half note receives beats or 3 counts.

o	This is a whole note the head is hallow it does not have a stem.	o	= 4 Beats a whole note will receive 4 beats or counts.

Remarks

At this point students should recognize the two added notes below the staff, C & D.

RESTS

A REST is a sign used to designate a period of silence.

This period of silence will be of the same duration of time as the note to which it corresponds.

 This is a QUARTER REST.

This is a HALF REST. Note that it lays on the line.

This is a WHOLE REST. Note that it hangs down from the line.

NOTES

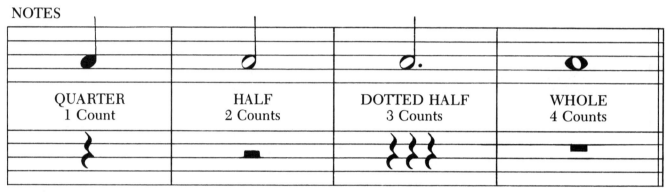

| QUARTER
1 Count | HALF
2 Counts | DOTTED HALF
3 Counts | WHOLE
4 Counts |

RESTS

Bar—lines divide the staff into measures.

THE TIME SIGNATURE

The above examples are the common types of time signatures to be used in this book.

4 The top number indicates the number of beats per measure.

4 The bottom number indicates the type of note receiving one beat.

3 Beats per measure

4 A quarter-note receives one beat

 Signifies so called "common time" and is simply another way of designating $\frac{4}{4}$ time.

THE RUDIMENTS OF MUSIC

THE STAFF: Music is written on a STAFF consisting of FIVE LINES and FOUR SPACES. The lines and spaces are numbered upward as shown:

5TH LINE	
4TH LINE	4TH SPACE
3RD LINE	3RD SPACE
2ND LINE	2ND SPACE
1ST LINE	1ST SPACE

THE LINES AND SPACES ARE NAMED AFTER LETTERS OF THE ALPHABET

The LINES in the Treble Clef are named as follows:

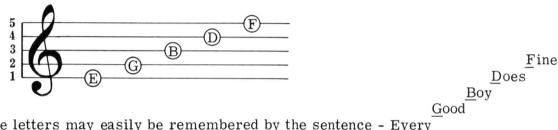

The letters may easily be remembered by the sentence - Every Good Boy Does Fine

The letter-names of the SPACES in the Treble Clef are:

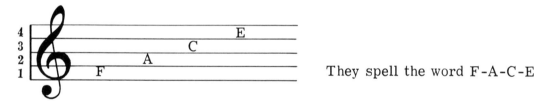

They spell the word F-A-C-E

The musical alphabet has seven letters — A   B   C   D   E   F   G

The STAFF is divided into measures by vertical lines called BARS.

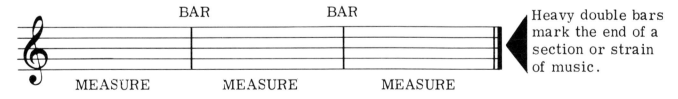

Heavy double bars mark the end of a section or strain of music.

RIGHT HAND CLEF

This sign is the treble or G clef.

LEFT HAND CLEF

This sign is the Bass or F clef.

FIRST FINGER C NOW HAS A NEW LOOK

The old

The - new

The new first finger C has a duration of three counts. Second finger D and third finger E will look the same and they will also receive three counts.

Study –

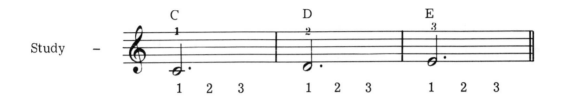

LETS PLAY

Open below on the top

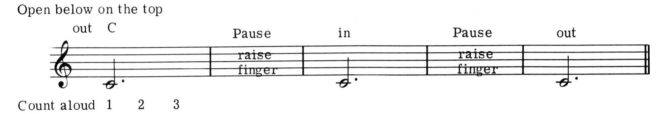

Count aloud 1   2   3

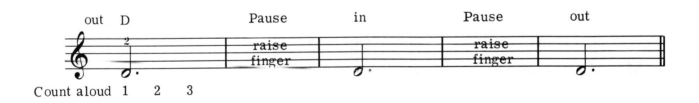

Count aloud 1   2   3

Count aloud 1   2   3

Check Point

Students should continue to find the two black keys without looking. Maintain a good hand position and a steady and even in and out bellow motion.

BASS CLEF SIGN

This sign is called the bass clef. When this sign appears, it means for the accordionist to play the left hand or the bass buttons.

The bass side of the accordion consists of two characters. The bass row sounds like one big C note played with the third finger. The chord row sounds like a variety of tones and is played with the second finger.

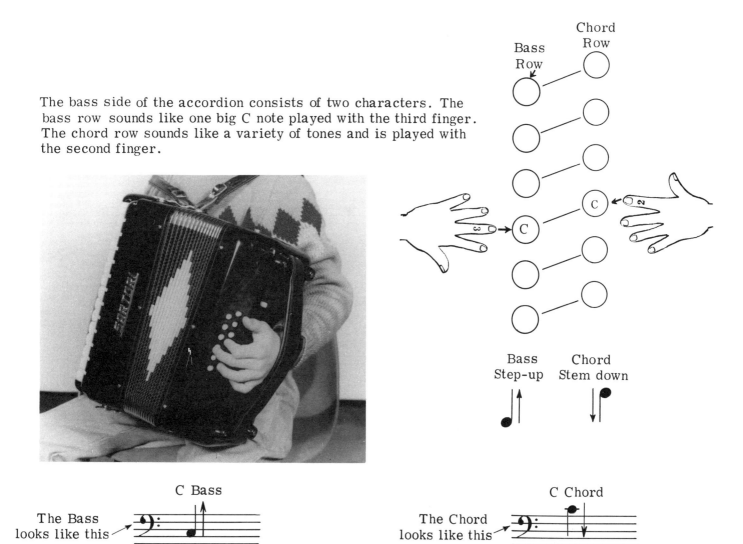

The Bass looks like this → C Bass
3
The stem goes up

The Chord looks like this → C Chord
2
Stem goes down

Check - Point

Check the position of the hand and fingers. The second and third fingers should remain well curved at all times. Do not permit the fingers to bend at the first joint when playing. The fingers should remain slightly above the bass and chord when releasing the buttons. The bass straps should be adjusted to hold the hand snugly against the bass board grill. The instructor can be of great help at this point. Remember, when playing with the left hand, maintain a steady in and out bellow motion. Do not use a jerky or abrupt motion.

𝄢 LETS PLAY 𝄢
The Third Finger C Base For Three Counts

Produce a steady and even tone.

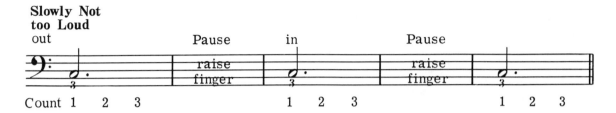

Third Finger C Base for One Count

The following notes of one count should be made very short.

The Mixer

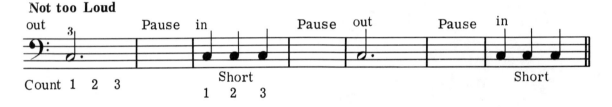

No Pause Mixer

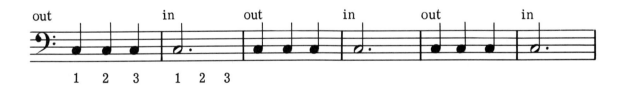

Check Point

The term "counting with the bellow" refers to a mistake often made by beginners. That is, jerking the bellow in or out on each count. This is frequently done when playing with the left hand alone. Remember, the bellow should be in a continuous motion at all times going out as well as coming in. Poor bellow control will be very noticeable when combining both hands. Once again, remember that control of the bellow is at the very heart of good accordion performance.

𝄢 MORE LEFT HAND 𝄢
The Second Finger C Chord For Three Counts

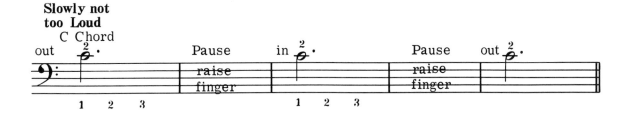

Second Finger C Chord for One Count

The following notes of one count should be made very short.

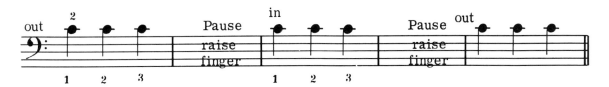

The Mixer

No Pause Mixer

Check Point

All notes of one count should be made very short. The second and third fingers should remain well rounded directly and slightly above the bass buttons. Make certain, however, that they are not touching the bass buttons.

✑: LEFT HAND CONTINUED ✑:
Second Finger C Chord

NO PAUSE BASS CHORD
Short and Snappy

𝄞 RIGHT HAND REVIEW 𝄞
First Finger C Second Finger D

✑: LEFT HAND ✑:
Snappy and Short

𝄞 RIGHT HAND 𝄞

Master the above before continuing on.

COMBINING BOTH HANDS
Remarks

The author believes that the time spent on the previous pages which involve playing with each hand separately is time well spent. Some teachers may desire, in order to move at a faster pace, to begin with both hands together. The following studies combine both hands.

RIGHT THAN LEFT

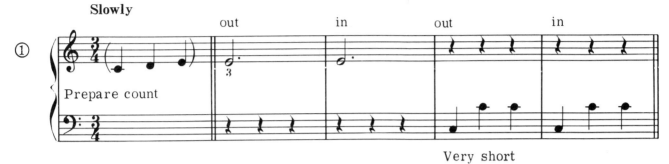

E AND C

E AND C TOGETHER

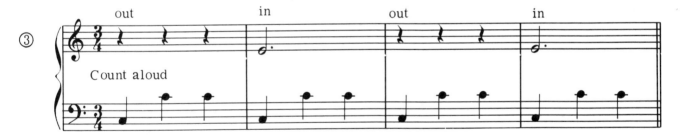

R-U-READY

Repeat the above studies as often as necessary especially no.3.

BOTH HANDS CONTINUED
C and E

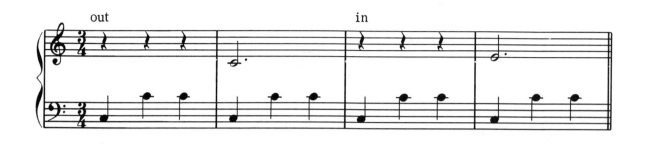

C - E - C -

𝄢 A NEW BASS 𝄢
Third Finger G Bass Second Finger G Chord

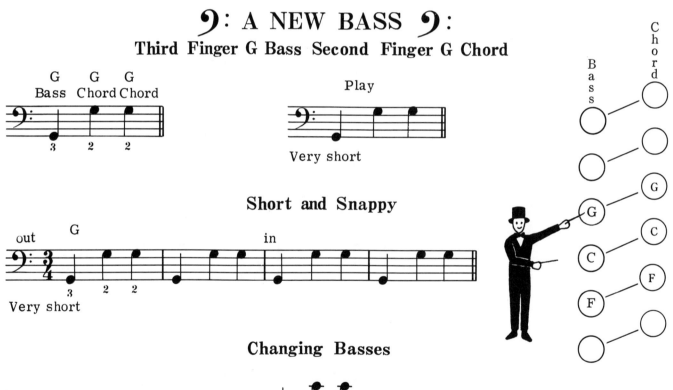

Short and Snappy

Changing Basses

Check Point

The fingers should remain will rounded above the bass buttons. Maintain a steady and even bellow movement.

G 𝄢 AND D 𝄞

Proceed in the same manner as on the proceeding page.

Softly

Solo Left Hand

BASS AND CHORD PLAYED TOGETHER

When the bass and the chord are on the same stem, play them together. This usually occurs at the end of a piece.

Mixer No. 1

Mixer No. 2

4TH FINGER F

Maintain a good hand position and steady bellow movement.

Slowly A-SHORT-TRIP

A-LONG-TRIP

𝄢 A NEW BASS 𝄢
Third Finger F Bass—Second Finger F Chord

F Bass F Chord F Chord

Play

Very short

Short and Snappy

out

Solo Bass Chord - Chord

CONCERT WALTZ
Deceptive

No-bellow markings

Check Point

At this point, the student should become acquainted with the names of all of the bass buttons. The instructor can supply any questions and details about the B Flat. Learning the names of the lines and spaces and the different types of notes and the time values associated with notes is also very important. Be sure to go back over this material many times.

A - NEW NOTE G

5th finger G

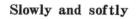

Study the picture carefully - notice the well curved fingers

PINKEY WALTZ

Slowly and softly

Count aloud

A review of the five basic notes write in the letter names above each note.

A review of the three basic basses and chords play and say.

NO - 1 - MIXER
Play and Say aloud

THE HOCKEY PUCK

NO - 2 - MIXER
Play and Say aloud

THE GOALIE

MIXER NO - 3

STACCATO VERSUS SLURRING
(Short Tones)   (Connected Tones)

Learning to slur quarter notes on the right hand while playing short or staccato quarter notes on the left hand can be a real challenge for the beginning student. This is a very important phase of accordion technique and should be mastered as soon as possible.

The Slur

A curved line ⌒ or ‿ connecting notes that are to be played in one continuous direction or motion of the bellow.

Examples

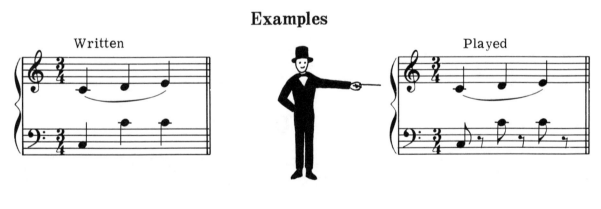

(Master the above examples before continuing)

When combining both hands, the quarter note in the bass should be held approximately one-half of the length of the quarter note in the right hand.

Examples

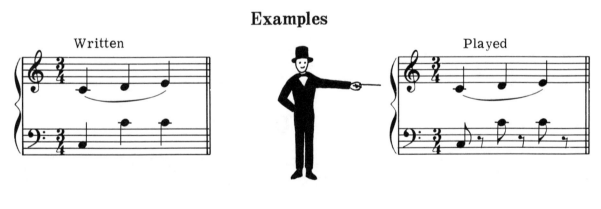

Warm Up

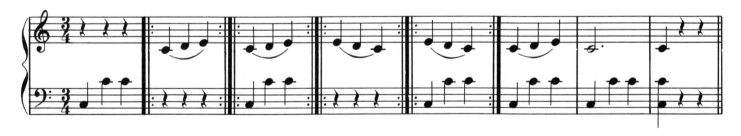

Remarks

To produce a good sound, students need to be taught to play the bass and chords short and snappy. Introducing the slur will help the student to gain independence of both hands and prevent playing short quarter notes in both hands at all times. In addition, introducing staccato versus slurring will, once again, help develop good bellow control and technique.

A CHANGE OF TIME

Study the following examples. Play and count them aloud 𝄞 here are same mixed rhythms in 4/4 time 𝄞 .

Count

1 2 3 4   1 2 3 4   1 2 3 4   1 2 3 4   1 2 3 4   1 2 3 4

𝄢 LEFT HAND BASS PATTERNS 𝄢
4/4 Time

Play Base Chord Base Chord

Short

Play Base Chord Chord Chord

Short

MIXER - NO - 1
𝄢 Left Hand Mixer 𝄢

Count aloud

Short

MIXER - NO - 2

Short

MIXER - NO - 3

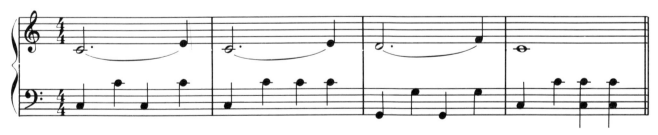

Bellow markings have been purposely omitted. Continue to play basses and chords short and snappy. Maintain a steady and even bellow motion at all times.

The bellow is the heart of the accordion.

THE TIE

A tie is a curved line which connects two notes of the same pitch or of the same line or space. The first note is played and held for the time duration of both notes. The second note is not played. It is just held and counted.

Examples

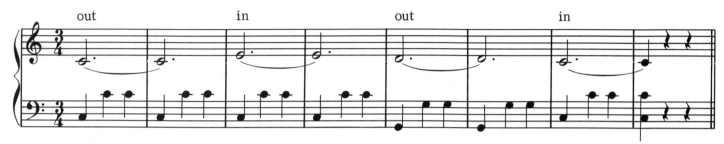

Changing the direction of the bellow is prohibited until the tie and the time value of both notes have been completed.

TIE-WALTZ

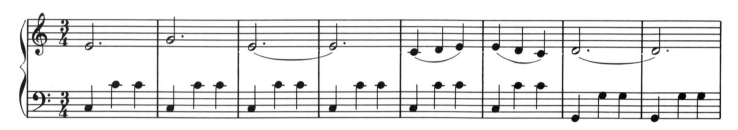

BELLOW CONTROL STUDIES

Practice the following studies in two ways ① - 2 measures out 2 in. ② - 4 measures out and 4 in.

FOUR AND FOUR

Written

Played

Bass notes half as long as the right hand notes.

TAG - A - LONG

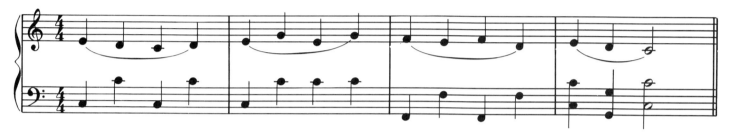

FOREIGN SONG

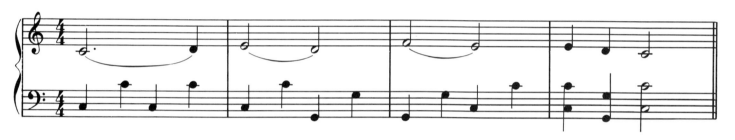

Check Point

Repeating the same note for one count with the right hand (quarter notes) and playing short quarter notes in the bass can be a real challenge to the student. This problem should be solved as soon as possible. We will use the following marking (–). This marking is called a legato marking. It will mean to play the right hand note for the full count.

Written

Played

OH BOY !

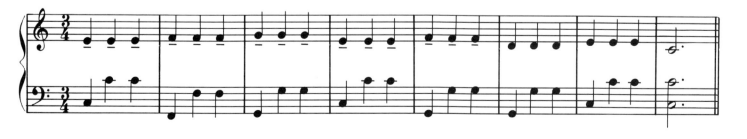

29

THE D POSITION

Memorize The Following

D is the white key between the two black keys. E is the white key after the two black keys. F is the white key before the three black keys or in the big space between the black keys. G is the next white key up. A is one white key further than the G key. Look at the picture for the exact location.

Find The D Key (Without Looking)

The right arm should be lowered at your side. Raise the hand up and grasp the two black keys between the first and third fingers. Slide the thumb over the first black key thus placing the thumb between the two black keys on the D note. Master this movement. When playing, the hand may be moved out and away from the black keys. Occasionally check the hand for the D position by moving the thumb between the two black keys.

Warm Up

Slowly

A NEW - BASS D

D bass and D chord looks like this

D POSITION CONTINUED
Bennies Twister

Carl Czeck

The Organ Player

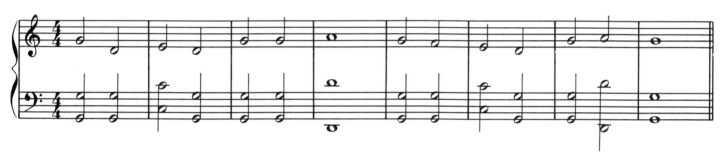

BLUES IN C
D Position

SMOKY
The Mouse Colored Pony

A-BIT-OF-HANNON

THE CHALLENGER

Check Point

Continue to play legato right hand and staccato left hand maintaining a steady inward and outward bellow motion.

SKATING

Smooth skating

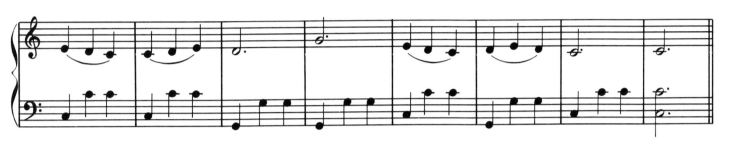

FINGER - DRILL
Elbow out-and-Up Hand Position Curved Fingers

out   in   out   in

GLIDER - WALTZ

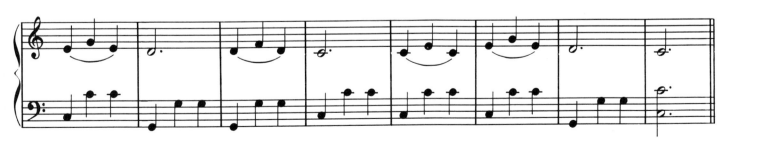

E-POSITION

Find the key (without looking)

Find the C key as explained on page 6. To find the E key, move the thumb over the top of the first black key, then over the top of the second black key. The thumb is now resting over the E key. The hand may be moved out and away from the black keys when playing.

E is the White Key-After the Two Black Keys

E Position

Warm-Up for the E-Position

Etude - No-1

Etude - No - 2

Roller Coaster

Check Point

Review finding the C and D position. Remember to look at the keyboard as little as possible in order to get a feel for where the notes are. Try to get a good mental picture of the keyboard. Remember also to maintain an even inward and outward bellow motion. Count time aloud in order to gain proper time values. Finally, practice all examples slowly until they can be played correctly.

E POSITION CONTINUED

WALTZ KING

KICK - POLKA

THE F POSITION
Find the F Key (Without Looking)

In order to find the F position, raise the right hand and grasp the three black keys between the first and third fingers. The thumb should now be on the F key. Look at the picture for proper positioning.

F Position

Etude - No - 1

Etude - No - 2

Rolie Coaster

The - Virtuoso Study

Check Point

Maintain a good hand position at all times. Make sure that the fingers are curved and that the elbow is up and out. Only the finger being used should actually touch the key. All other fingers should be raised above the appropriate keys.

F POSITION CONTINUED
I-Hate Spinach
Waltz

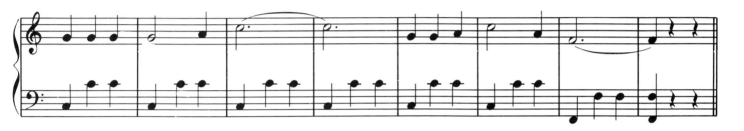

Beethoven-9th-Symphony-
Theme

The Fighting-Sea Bees
March

FIRST AND SECOND ENDINGS

Sometimes two endings are required in certain selections.. one to lead back into a repeated chorus and one to close it.

They will be shown like this.

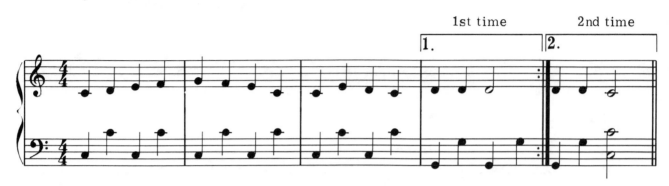

The first time play the bracketed ending 1. Repeat the chorus. The second time skip the first ending and play ending no.2.

CHOPSTICKS

Repeat from the begining

[Instructor play the small added notes.]

PICK-UP NOTES

The notes at the beginning of a strain before the first measure are referred to as pick-up notes. The rhythm for pick-up notes is taken from the last measure of the selection and the beats are counted as such. (Note the two beats in the last measure.)

Scout-Patrol March
Three Pick Up Notes

Moon-Patrol-March
Two Pick Up Notes

Roll-Call
One Pick Up Notes

Check-Point

✳ B♭ Bass and chord is one below F Bass and F chord.

FEEL AND TOUCH
A Positive Guide for Finding the White Keys

In the diagram below, the dot shows where to place the fingers between the black keys. The most commonly used fingers for making skips (ascending) are fingers 1-2, 1-3, 1-4, 1-5. The most commonly used fingers for making descending jumps are fingers 2-1, 3-1, 4-1. It is not necessary to continue to play between the black keys. After finding the proper key or note, the hand may be moved out and away from the black keys.

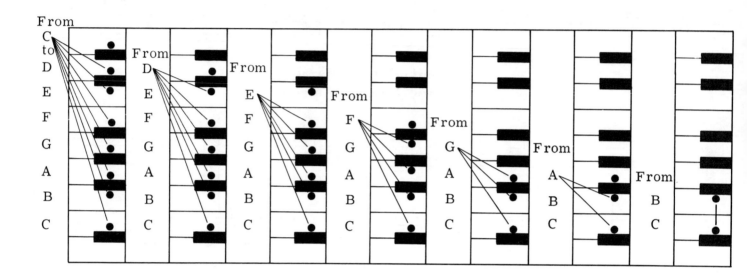

The above diagram illustrates skips ascending. For skips descending reverse the procedure. The fingers may remain between the black keys when the music has a succession of skips. Sliding the finger lightly over the black keys can also be a great help for finding the proper white keys.

Memorize the Following

C is the white key before the two black keys

D . . . . between . . . .

E . . . . after . . . .

F . . . . before the three black keys

G and A are white keys between the three black keys .

B is the white key after the three black keys.

MORE ABOUT FEEL AND TOUCH

Practice the following studies between the black keys and do not look at the keyboard.
Try to get a good mental picture of the keyboard, especially the group containing the two and
three black keys. Visualize also the big space between E and F and B and C.

Check Point

Mastering the above studies will be time well spent.

♯ THE SHARP SIGN ♯

A sharp sign placed before a note raises the pitch one half step. Play the nearest black key up.

F to F♯

D Position

D Position, 5, Fingers

Warm up

42

♭ THE FLAT SIGN ♭

A flat sign placed before a note lowers the pitch one half step. Play the nearest black key back.

B to B♭

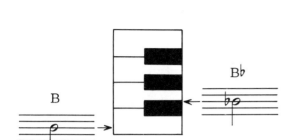

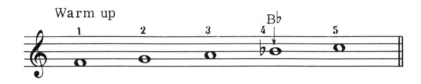

F Position 5 Fingers

B♭ Drill

LIGHTLY ROW

MERRILY WE ROLL ALONG

SUMMER TIME

GOING HOME

JINGLE BELLS

SECOND C POSITION

The second C position is above the first C position and is found in the middle of the keyboard. In order to find it raise the right hand and grasp the two black keys in the middle of the keyboard. Do not look at the keyboard when finding it. Grasp the two black keys between the first and third fingers. The keys will be arranged in the same manner as were found in the low C position. The only difference now is that the notes will be higher on the staff and located in a higher position on the keyboard. Look at the diagram for proper positioning of second C position.

12 - Bass Keyboard

First C position

First C positon

Second C position

Second C position

ECHO - WALTZ

SECOND C-POSITION CONTINUED
Top o'the Morning

KITCHEN DANCE

Strong–beat
Not too fast

SAINTS

EIGHTH NOTES AND EIGHTH RESTS

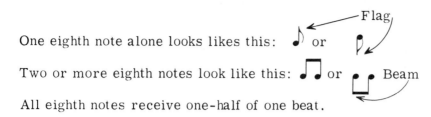

One eighth note alone looks likes this: ♪ or

Two or more eighth notes look like this: ♫ or

All eighth notes receive one-half of one beat.

An eighth rest looks like this: ♪

It also receives one-half of a beat.

Counting the Eighth Notes

Clap the hands in a steady upward and downward movement.

By playing a note on the downbeat and a note on the upbeat, you are actually playing two notes per beat - eighth notes.

COUNT ALOUD

Clap the hands in a steady even down up movement.

Etude - No - 1

Etude - No - 2

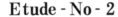

Etude - No - 3

Etude - No - 4

OH! BOY

Solve this riddle and you might receive a gold fiddle!

EIGHTH NOTES COTINUED
Combining Both Hands

Count the rhythm aloud as written for the right hand. (Do not play.)

Count only ——→

1 & 2 & 3 & 4 & 1 & 2 & 3 4 1 & 2 3 & 4

Play ——→

Written

Played

CHECK - MATE

Basses short

FOLK - SONG

Slowly

Basses short

SKIPPY

ITALIAN FOLK SONG

DANCING CLOWN

MARCHING SONG

To play the next melody it becomes necessary to move the thumb down one key out of the five finger position. Practice the following exercise as preparation for polka time.

POLKA TIME

THEORY LESSONS
Check-Point

Draw   4 Treble clefs _____

4 Bass clefs _____

4 Sharps _____

4 Flats _____

4 Whole notes _____

4 Dotted half notes _____

4 Half notes _____

4 Quarter notes _____

6 Eight notes - (Flag _____

6 Eight notes - (Beam _____

4 Whole rests

4 Half rests

4 Quarter rests

4 Eight rests

name this

How many beats in a measure in 4/4 time _____

How many beats in a measure in 3/4 time _____

How many beats in a measure in 2/4 time _____

Draw the counts under the following notes

Draw the counts under the following notes

Congratulations! You are now in level
two of the Mel Bay Accordion Method.

REMINDERS

1. Make certain that you have good bellow control.

2. Keep counting time aloud to make certain that your time values are correct.

3. Use the black keys as an aide for finding the white keys. This is especially helpful on skips and jumps. Refer back to pages 40 and 41 often.

4. Play your bass and chords short and snappy. Do not allow the sound to linger on.

5. Most important! Practice everyday.

JOLLY COPPERSMITH

C Peter

ALTERNATING THE BASSES

Any bass may be used alternately say the names aloud

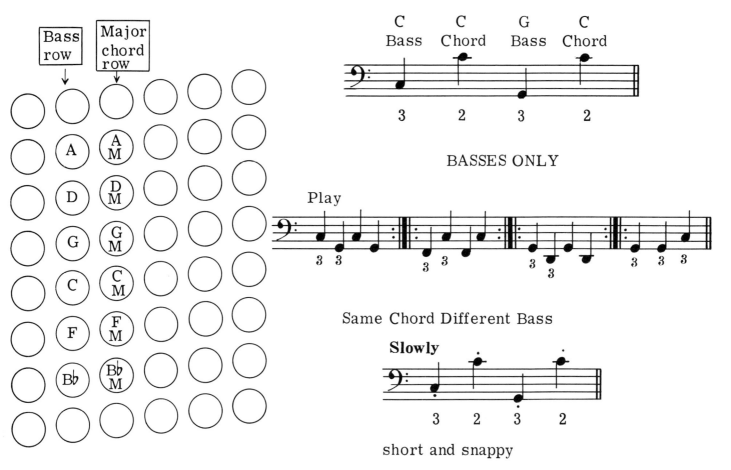

BASSES ONLY

Same Chord Different Bass

Slowly

short and snappy

Alternating the basses is a more advanced way of playing the left hand

and it also produces a better sound.

PREPARATORY STUDIES
FOR ALTERNATING BASSES

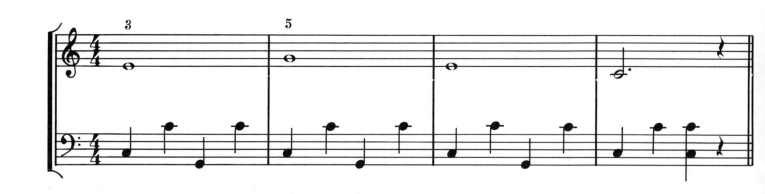

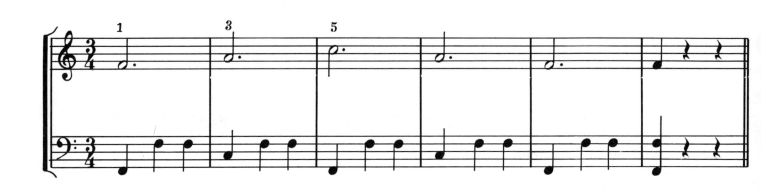

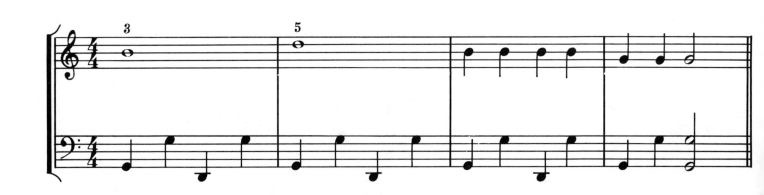

WINTER SPORTS

March time not too fast

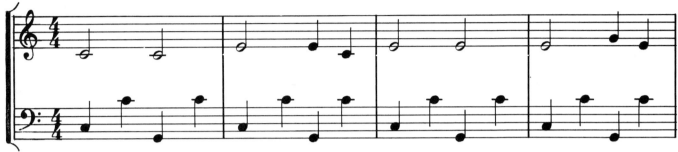

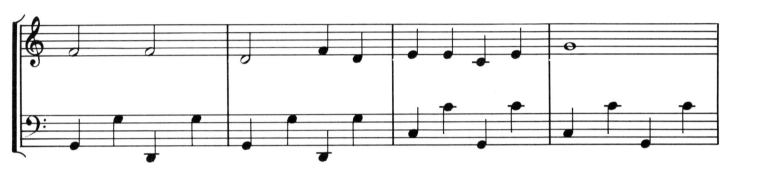

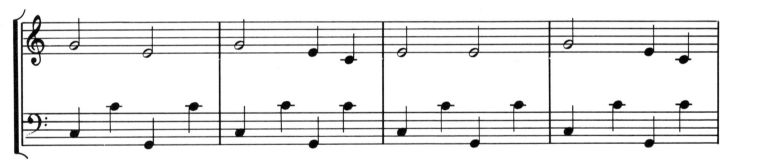

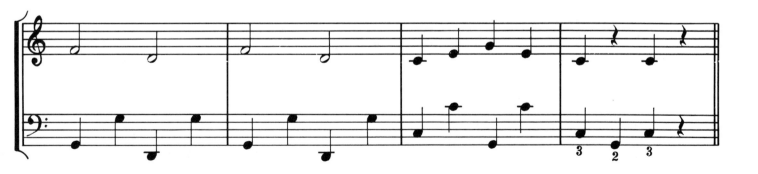

UM PA PA POLKA

F.C.Z.

"Expression" - marks

   (forte) = Loud

   (mezzo-forte)= Moderatly loud

   (piano) = Soft

- Tempo -

Tempo is the rate of speed

Andante - a slow Easy pace

Moderato - Moderate

Allegro - Lively

DRINK TO ME WITH ONLY THINE EYES

Old English

ROCK-N-BLUES

MUSICAL TERMS

Dynamics

DYNAMIC markings indicate the degree of loudness and softness to be used when playing.

cresc. or ═══◁ ....crescendo... gradually getting louder

decresc. or ▷═══ ....decrescendo or diminuendo...gradually getting softer

ff ....fortissimo...very loud

f ....forte...loud

mf ...mezzo-forte...moderately loud

mp ...mezzo-piano...moderately soft

p ....piano...softly

pp ....pianissimo...very soft

Tempo

TEMPO markings indicate the rate of speed at which a composition is to be played.

Accelerando (accel.) ....growing faster
Adagio...........................slowly, leisurely
Allegretto........lively; faster than andante, slower than allegro
Allegro ....lively and fast
Andante.................a moderately slow but flowing tempo
Andantino....... can mean both slower and faster than andante
Assai..very
Grave....................very slow and solemn
Larghetto............a little faster than Largo
Largo.................slow, broad, and stately
Lento.....slow; between andante and largo
Meno Mosso...............less motion; slower
Moderato.....................a moderate speed

Style

STYLE markings indicate the manner in which a piece is to be played.

Animato ....with spirit
A tempo.......................in the original tempo
Dolce...sweetly
Espressivo....................................expressively
Grandioso...........................in a grand manner
Legato...........................smoothly, connected
Leggiero...lightly
Maestoso.....................majestic and dignified
Marcato...............marked, and with emphasis
Non troppo.............................not too much
Poco...little
Rall. (rallentando).... gradually getting slower
Rit. (ritardando)....... gradually getting slower
Simile...................similarly; in a like manner
Staccato.........................separated, detached
Tenuto.......................held out to full value

MINUET-BACH 4/4 VERSION

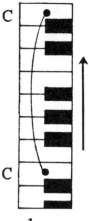

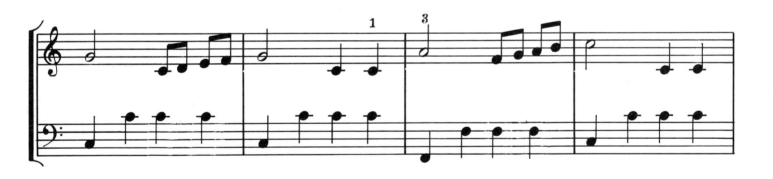

HAPPY MOMENTS
MAZURKA

F.C.Z.

Tempo de mazurka

THE SCALE

A scale is a succession of tones ascending and descending in regular order. A scale is made up of whole steps and half steps. E to F and B to C are two half steps. They are found in the large space which separates the black keys. These half steps are called "diatonic half steps".

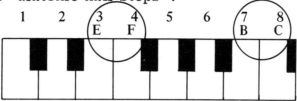

Important Rules For Playing The Scale

ASCENDING

Maintain a good hand position. The fingers should be well curved. When the second finger strikes the key, pass the thumb under. It remains underneath until the F key is played. The first finger continues on to F, the second finger on to G, the third finger on to A, the fourth finger on to B, and the fifth finger on to C.

DESCENDING

C-5, B-4, A-3, G-2, F-1. Pass the third finger over the top to E-3, D-2, C-1?

LET'S PLAY

thumb
under

over
the top

CHECKPOINT

Play the scale with a smooth and connected touch (legato), especially when going from E-3, F-1 ascending and F-1, E-3 descending. Watch for the scarecrow. The scarecrow will be used as a help and a reminder in learning and reviewing musical concepts.

PREPARATION FOR PLAYING "CAN CAN"

After finding the second C, the hand may be moved out and away from the black keys.

CAN CAN

THE CAMPTOWN RACES

S. Foster

Not too fast

DOTTED QUARTER NOTE

♩. = One and one half beats

A dot after a quarter note increases its value by one half.

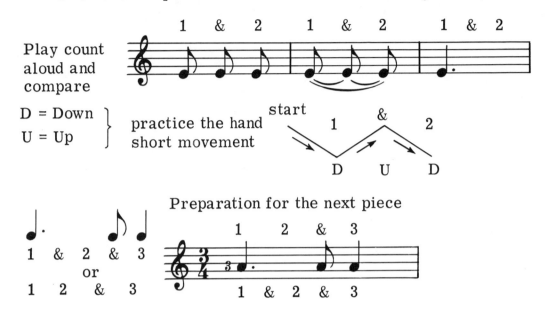

Play count
aloud and
compare

D = Down
U = Up } practice the hand short movement

Preparation for the next piece

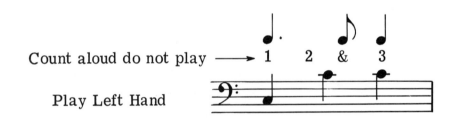

Count aloud do not play ⟶

Play Left Hand

Practice the following examples.

Possible rhythm patterns

COUNTRY GARDENS

Reveiw C Major Scale

English

D.C. al Fine

D.C. al Fine = Go back to the beginning and play to fine.

KEY SIGNATURES

The key signature is that part of the staff which is reserved for indicating which sharps and flats are to be played throughout the piece.

HERE ARE SOME EXAMPLES

Key of C no sharps or flats the sharps

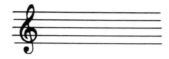

F sharp

Key of G one sharp - F sharp

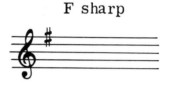

F-sharp and C sharp

Key of D two sharps = F♯ - C♯

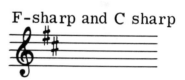

THE -FLATS

B flat

Key of F one flat B flat

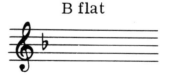

B flat and E flat

Key of B flat = B flat and - E flat

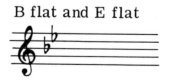

CHECKPOINT

From this point on all sharps and flats will be indicated in the key signature at the beginning of the piece.

LARGO

A. Dvorak

A REVIEW OF
SHARPS, FLATS, AND NATURALS
LET US REVIEW THE FOLLOWING RULES:

1. A sharp (♯) before a note raises the pitch one half step-next black key up

2. A flat (♭) before a note lowers the pitch one half step-one black key back

3. A natural (♮) before a note restores it to its original pitch or key

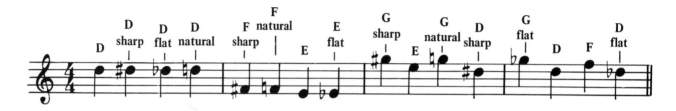

Name the following notes below aloud

Place the letter names in the square, the sharps or flats in the circle.

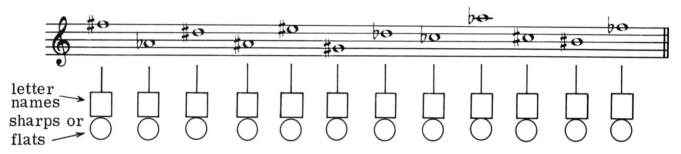

AN IMPORTANT RULE

A sharp, flat, or natural sign placed before a note remains in effect for the duration of the measure unless notes that follow are marked otherwise by use of accidentals.

1. Notes that have been circled are still affected by the sharp signs.

2. Notes that have been circled are still affected by the flat signs.

3. Notes that are circled have been restored to their original pitch by naturals.

HALF STEPS

A half step is the smallest difference in pitch between any two musical sounds. It is also the distance from a black key to a white key or from a white key to a black key. Sharps, flats, and natural signs can be placed before all notes of the musical alphabet.

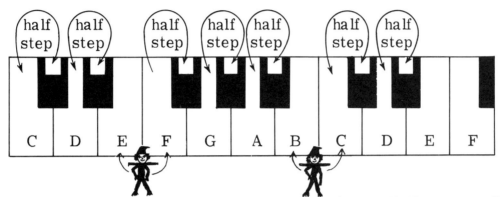

Study and compare the keyboard on the accordion with the proceeding picture.

- FLATS -   SHARPS

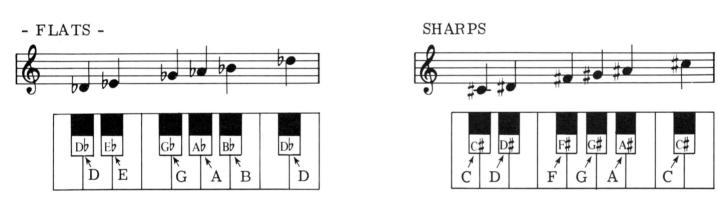

SECOND C POSITION

FLATS   SHARPS

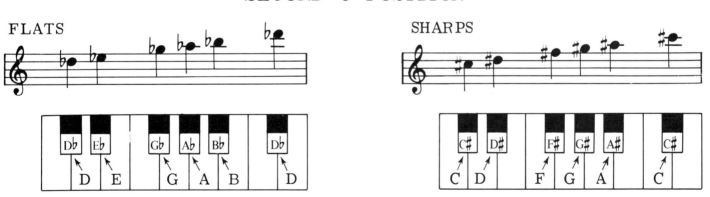

Half steps which are produced by the use of sharps and flats (black and white keys) are called chromatic half steps. The half steps between E and F, B and C (white keys), are called diatonic half steps. There is no black key needed for those half steps.

69

CARNIVAL OF VENICE

Italian

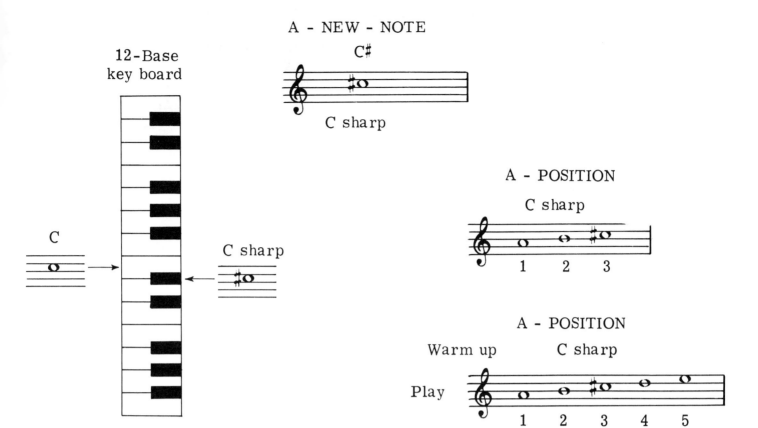

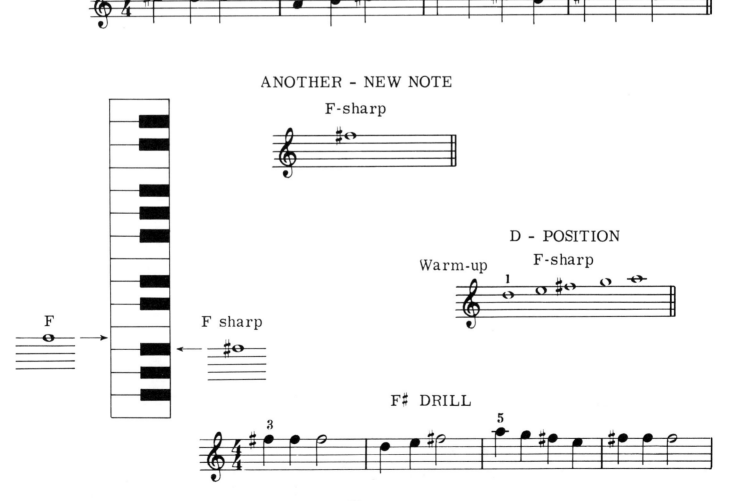

71

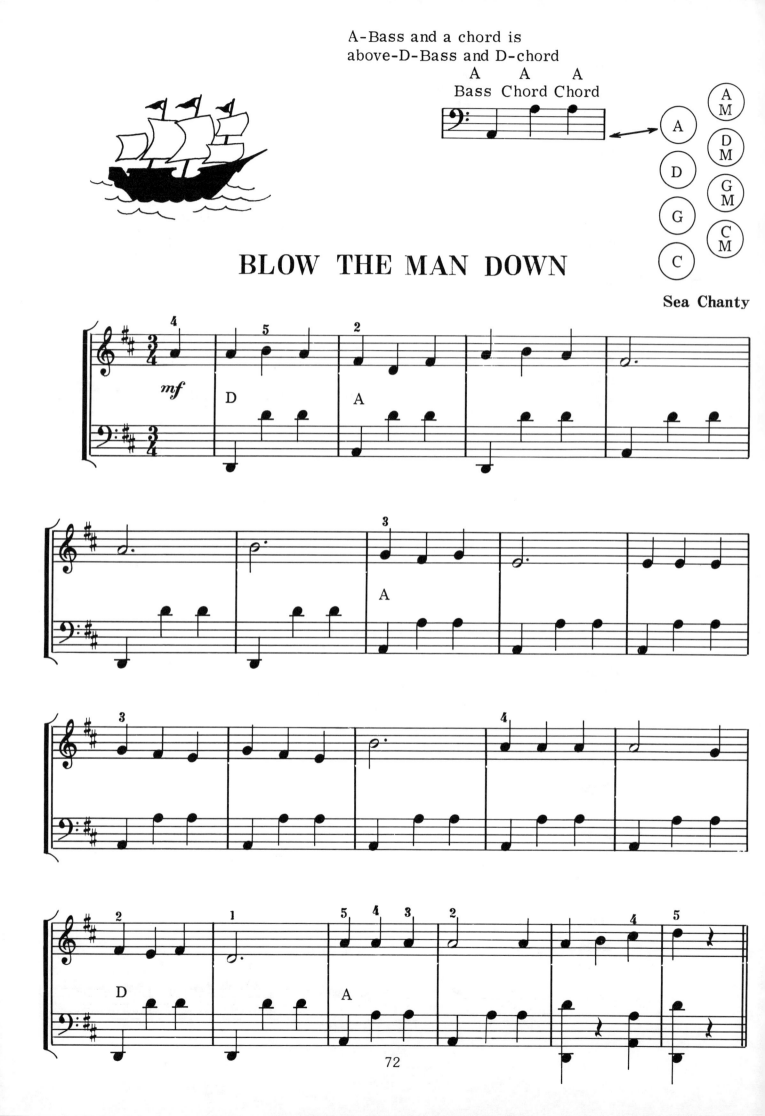

A-Bass and a chord is
above-D-Bass and D-chord

BLOW THE MAN DOWN

Sea Chanty

FURTHER EXPLANATION OF THE - BLACK KEYS
SHARPS AND FLATS

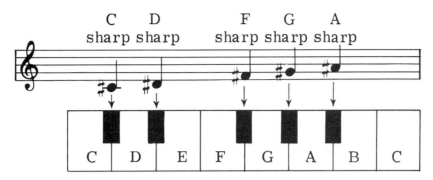

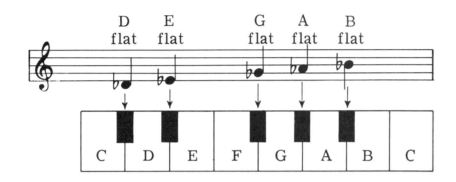

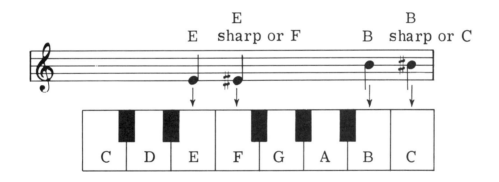

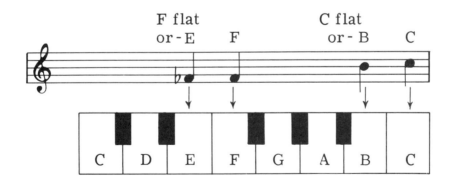

CHECKPOINT

At this point students may wonder about black keys not used thus far in this accordion method. The above examples should demonstrate the use of additional black keys. The teacher may need to explain in more detail about the enharmonic changes of E to E♯, F to F♭, B to B♯, and C to C♭.

WHOLE STEPS

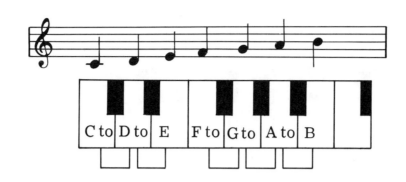

POSSIBLE WHOLE STEPS

PLAY THE FOLLOWING EXAMPLES

HALF STEPS AND MORE HALF STEPS
PRACTICE THE FALLOWING

PLAY AND COMPARE WITH THE ABOVE

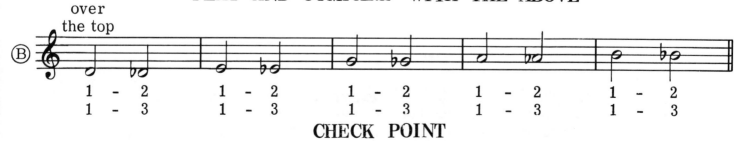

CHECK POINT

The above half steps may be played with a variety of fingerings.

LEVEL THREE

Before continuing on to level three, remember this very important word:

RECAPITULATE

It sometimes becomes necessary to go back and review (recapitulate). There are many things to remember. The bellow, counting, time, feel, and touch. We will not review the proceeding instructions so make sure you have learned them well and remember to "RECAPITULATE".

Level three will advance the student one half grade. It will introduce some pieces by many famous composers and will contain some very interesting new material.

RIGHT HAND OF THE 120-BASS ACCORDION

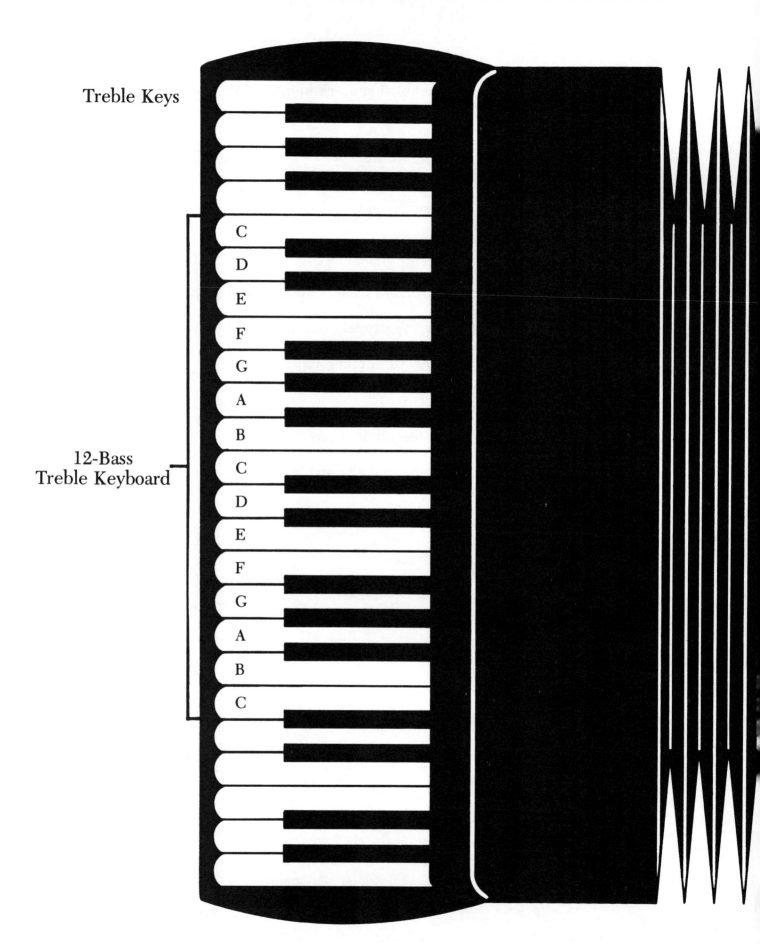

Treble Keys

12-Bass
Treble Keyboard

C
D
E
F
G
A
B
C
D
E
F
G
A
B
C

LEFT HAND OF THE 120-BASS ACCORDION

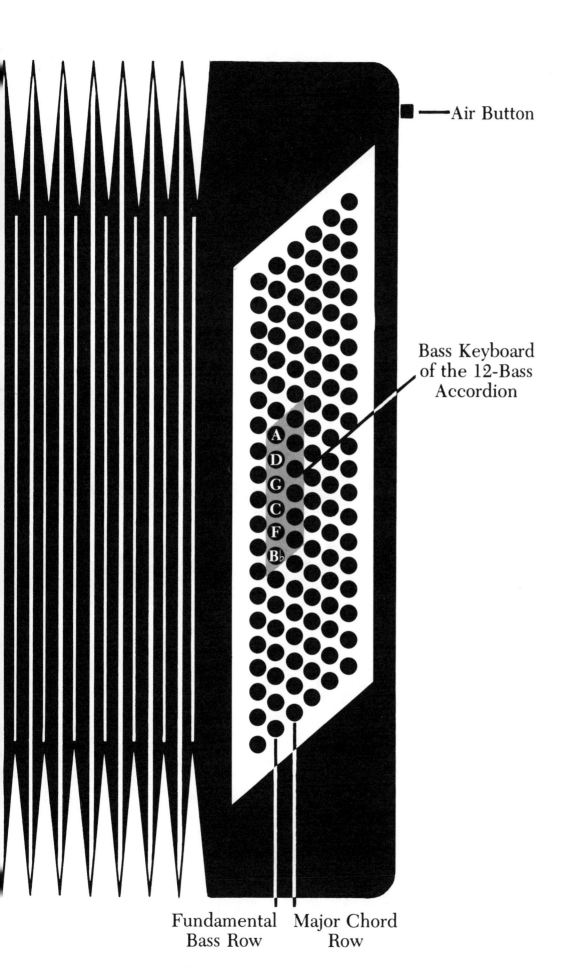

Air Button

Bass Keyboard
of the 12-Bass
Accordion

Fundamental
Bass Row

Major Chord
Row

SILVER SKATES

F.C.Z.

THIS OLD MAN

Traditional

MY DARLING CLEMENTINE

CHECKPOINT

Remember to play only slightly between the black keys. In the course of a tune it may become necessary to move the fingers in and away from the black keys many times, depending on the amount of skips and jumps contained in the song.

THREE DIATONIC MAJOR SCALES
G - MAJOR - F - SHARP

D - MAJOR - SCALE - F - SHARP - C - SHARP - EXTENTION

F - MAJOR - SCALE - B - FLAT

THE - SHEPHERD

W. Mozart

INTRODUCING THE COUNTER BASSES

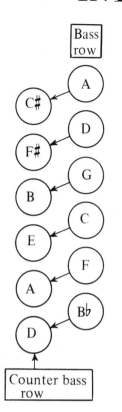

The row of basses nearest to the bellow is called the COUNTER BASS ROW. The counter basses and the bass row are principally used to play melodies and bass solos. Study and memorize the following:

Counter bass to C is E = Count up three notes C - D - E

Counter bass to G is B = Count up three notes G - A - B

Counter bass to D - F♯ = Count up three notes D - E - F♯ add a sharp

Counter bass to A - C♯ = Count up three notes A - B - C♯ add a sharp

Counter bass to F - A = Count up three notes F - G - A

Counter bass to B♭ - D = Count up three notes B♭ - C - D

Counter basses are indicated by a dash below the notes.

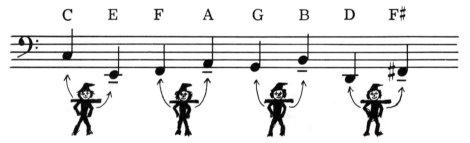

PREPARATION FOR PLAYING THE SCALE

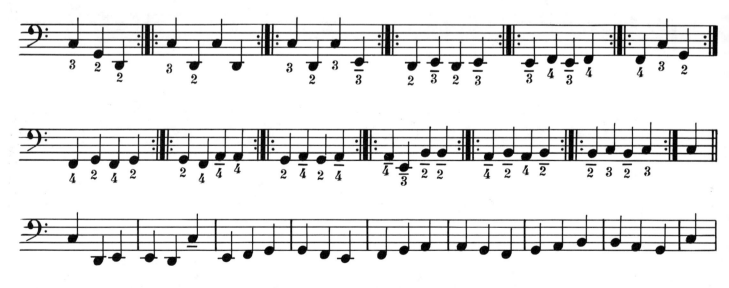

The C Major-Scale

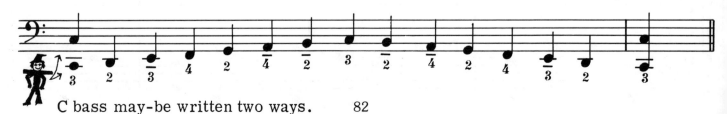

C bass may-be written two ways.   82

GOOD-NIGHT LADIES

Folk

THE MARINES HYMN

84

Position of the
fingers for playing
the seventh chord

THE SEVENTH CHORD

C Major = large M above the chord

C Minor - A small mi above the chord

The minor chord is introduced only as an
aid for finding the seventh chord.

C = 7th the figure 7 above the chord

ALTERNATING - BASS

THE GLOW WORM

Lincke

PRES. LINCOLN'S CAMPAIGN WALTZ

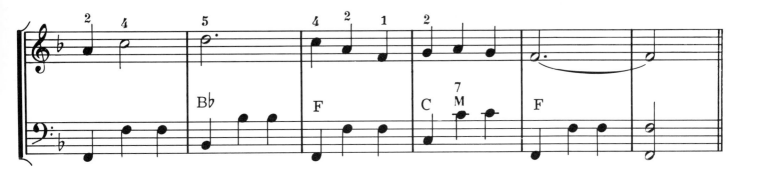

COME TO THE SEA

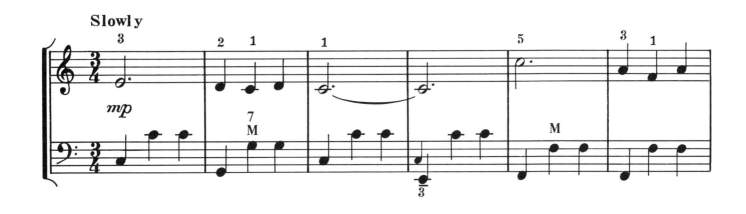

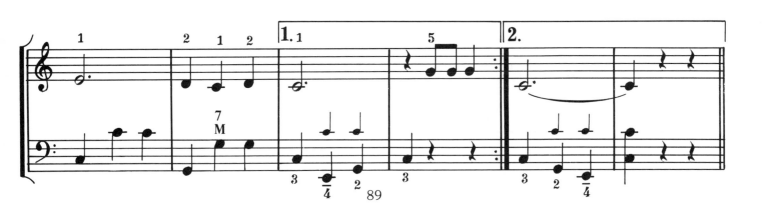

WHAT A FRIEND WE HAVE IN JESUS

Organ Style Left Hand
Chords Only

F. Converse

Moderato

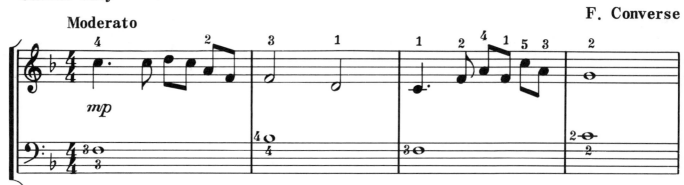

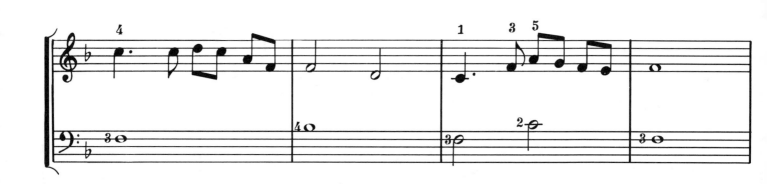

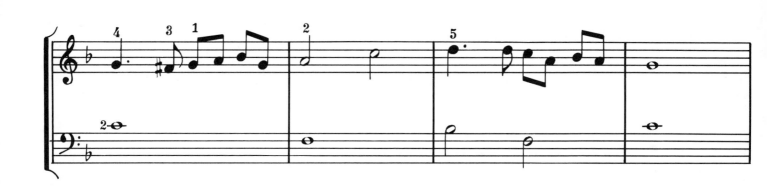

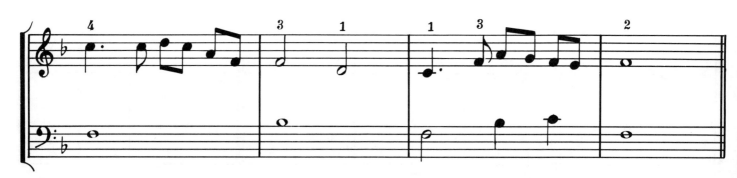

JET STREAM
FROLICKING HALF STEPS

JENNY LIND POLKA

CARELESS LOVE

Folk Song

TRIPLETS
(There notes of a kind played in equal value)

Eighth note triplets are written as above. An eighth note triplet contains three notes on a single beam with the figure "3" above or below the notes.

Play them the way you say them.

Count aloud clap the hands or tap on the music stand saying

1 tri-plet   2 tri-plet   3 tri-plet

Play and count aloud

WALTZING TRIPLETS

ETUDE

C. Czerny

Moderato

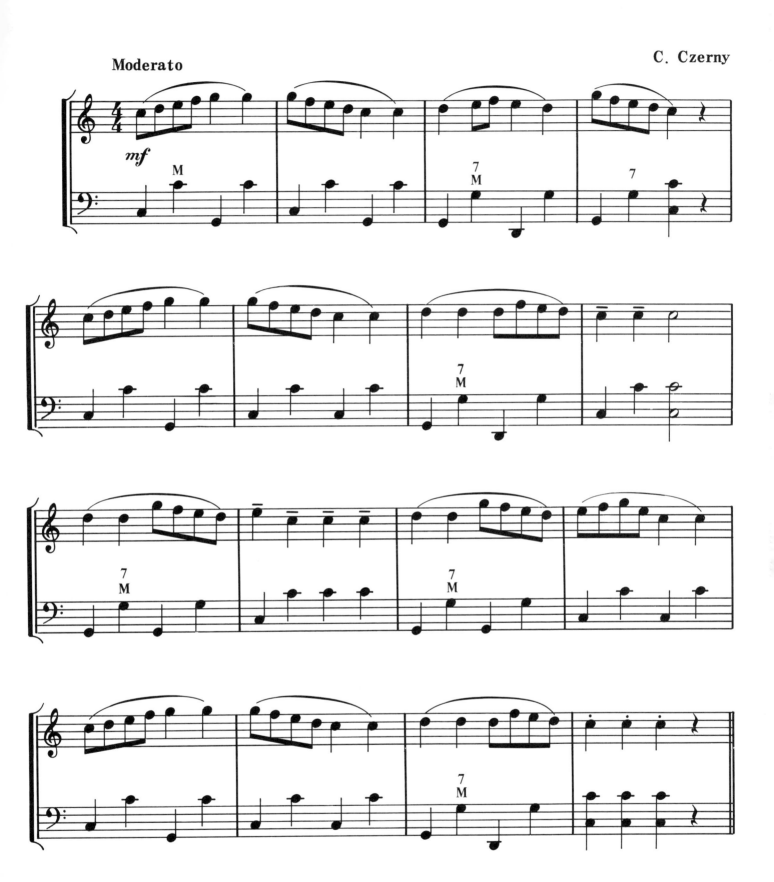

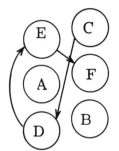

Using G-D-in
the counter bass row

Counter bass row

FRANKIE AND JOHNNY

THE MINOR-CHORD
MINOR A SMALL mi ABOVE THE CHORD
The minor chord is the next button behind the major chord
Preparation for Playing The Minor Chord

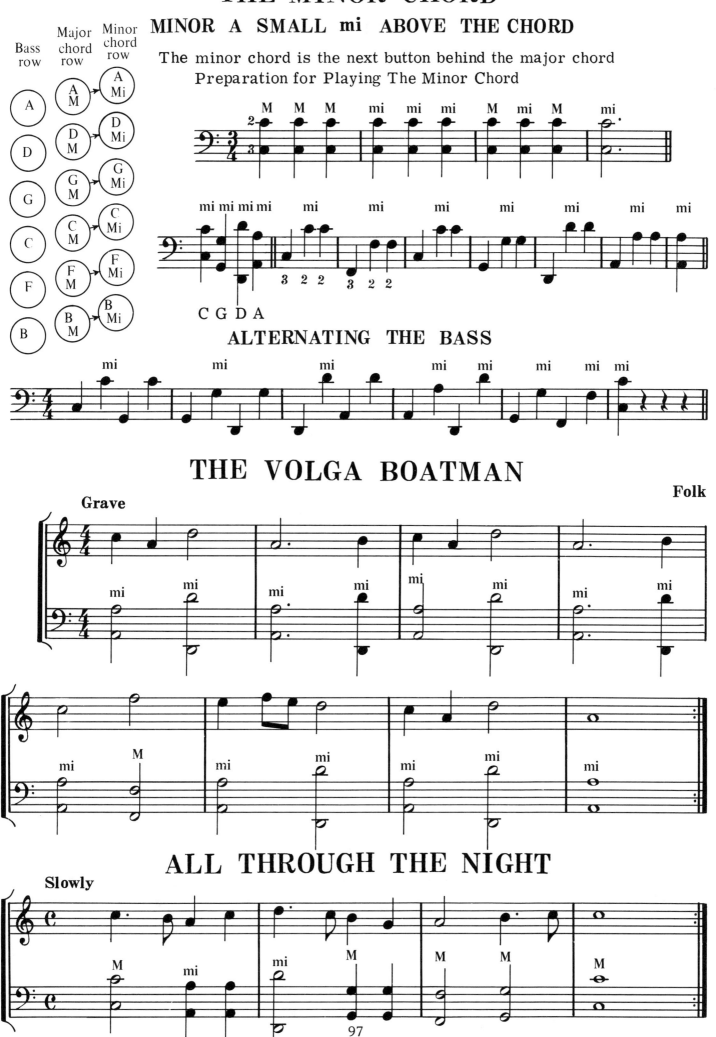

ALTERNATING THE BASS

THE VOLGA BOATMAN

Folk

Grave

ALL THROUGH THE NIGHT

Slowly

NORWEGIAN DANCE

E. Grieg

LEFT HAND OF THE 120-BASS ACCORDION

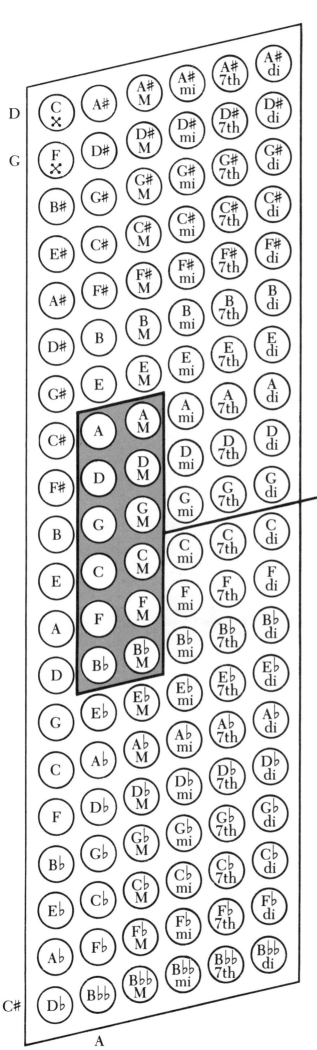

BASS
KEYBOARD
OF THE
12-BASS
ACCORDION

| Double Sharp = ⤬ |
| Double Flat = ♭♭ |
| Large M = Major |
| Small mi = Minor |
| 7th = 7th Chord |
| Small di = Diminished |

Great Music at Your Fingertips